GREAT MINDS® WIT & WISDOM

Grade 7 Module 3:
Language and Power

Student Edition

COPYRIGHT STATEMENT

ISBN: 978-1-68386-047-1

Table of Contents

Name _____

Date _____   Class _____

Handout 1A: Poetry Terms

Directions: Keep track of terms below, and use them to enrich your writing and discussion about poetry.

Term	Definition	Examples
figurative language (n.)	Words that are used to mean something other than or more than their literal meaning (for example, similes and metaphors).	
sensory language (n.)	Language that connects to the five senses (sight, sound, smell, taste, touch) to create an image or description.	
metaphor (n.)	A phrase that describes something by comparing it to some other thing.	
simile (n.)	A phrase that describes something by comparing it to some other thing using the words *like* or *as*.	
repetition (n.)	A device that repeats the same words or phrases to emphasize an idea.	

Term	Definition	Examples

Name _____

Date _____ Class _____

Handout 3A: Inspiration Cube

Directions: On each square, write the most inspiring quotation from each text your teacher indicates. Justify your choices in your Response Journal. After concluding your study of inspiring language, cut out the shape, fold along the lines, and tape the sides together to construct a cube.

Name _____

Date _____ Class _____

Handout 3B: Informative and Argument Paragraph Comparison

Directions: First, compare and contrast the paragraphs. Note that each part of ToSEEC is labeled in the informative paragraph. Then when your teacher gives the instruction, label each part of CREEA-C in the argument paragraph.

Informative Paragraph

ToS: Sarah Kay's "B" uses figurative language to express themes about life's joy and life's pain. **E:** In it, Kay addresses a hypothetical daughter, saying, "life will hit you hard...But getting the wind knocked out of you is the only way to remind your lungs how much they like the taste of air." **E:** Through personification of life and lungs, Kay shows that life can cause shocking pain. However, when Kay says this pain reminds lungs to enjoy air, she suggests that struggles can remind us to appreciate what we have. **C:** This language emphasizes Kay's message to enjoy life despite challenges.

Argument Paragraph

_____ : If one falls ill and must stay home on Friday night, the best way to pass the time is to watch figurative-language-filled spoken word poetry. _____ : Figurative language can uplift anyone's mood. _____ : For example, in "B," Sarah Kay uses figurative language to address a hypothetical daughter, saying, "life will hit you hard... But getting the wind knocked out of you is the only way to remind your lungs how much they like the taste of air." _____ : This line personifies life and lungs to demonstrate a truth that will comfort those who wish they could be out with friends: everyone experiences pain, but challenges can help us appreciate life's beauty. _____ : Some might claim that watching movies is a better activity because movies are relaxing. However, when one is feeling down, inspiration is more important than relaxation. _____ : For sick nights, the inspiring effect of figurative language in poetry like "B" cannot be topped.

Name _____

Date _____ Class _____

Handout 3C: Argument Paragraph and Essay Structures

Directions: Use the following structures to guide your argument writing.

Paragraph Version: CREEA-C

C	Claim	State your claim(s) about a topic.
R	Reason	State a reason that supports your claim.
E	Evidence	Cite evidence for the reason, including necessary context.
E	Elaboration	Explain how the evidence relates to the reason.
A	Alternate Claim(s) *	Acknowledge alternate or opposing claim(s).
C	Concluding Statement	Reinforce your argument.

Essay Version: HI-CREEA-CC

H	Hook	Catch your audience's attention.
I	Introduce	Introduce your audience to the topic.
C	Claim	State your claim(s) about the topic,
		and preview your supporting reasons.

R	Reason	State a reason that supports your claim.
E	Evidence	Cite evidence for the reason, including necessary context.
E	Elaboration	Explain how the evidence relates to the reason.
C	Concluding Statement	Close the paragraph.

	Reason	Transition from your last reason,	and state another reason that supports your claim.
	Evidence	Cite evidence for the reason, including necessary context.	
	Elaboration	Explain how the evidence relates to the reason.	
	Concluding Statement	Close the paragraph.	

A	Alternate Claim(s) *	Acknowledge alternate or opposing claim(s).

C	Conclusion	Reinforce your argument, reflecting on its significance.

*Acknowledgement of alternate or opposing claim(s) does not occur in a fixed order—it can happen anywhere in the paragraph or essay.

Name _____

Date _____ Class _____

Handout 3D: Academic Word Use

Directions: Decide which sentences involve an academic use of the words *argument* or *claim*, and mark those sentences with an A. If a sentence involves another usage of one of the words, mark the sentence with an O. If you are unsure of how a word is used, mark it with a U. Use Handout 3C as a reference as needed.

Sentences using *claim*:

_____ He filed a claim with the insurance company to have his medical bills repaid.

_____ The student claims that someone copied from his paper during the test.

_____ His classmates found his claim that the poem's dominant theme was that love conquers all unconvincing, because he was only able to point to one line in the poem to support his position.

_____ Her classmates found her claim that spoken word poetry is the best kind of poetry unconvincing, because they preferred other types of poems.

_____ The student claims that the dog ate his homework for the third time this week.

Sentences using *argument*:

_____ He had an argument with his uncle in which he gave him five reasons why he should be allowed to go to the party.

_____ She made a respectful argument to her teacher that students should be able to take notes on their laptops in class.

_____ The friends' argument about the best type of music turned ugly, and they were soon shouting at each other.

_____ Her classmates found themselves reconsidering their claims after hearing her argument; her reasoning was sound, and she had supported it with plenty of relevant evidence.

_____ You'll get no argument from me about that meal. I agree with you—it was delicious!

Name _____

Date _____   Class _____

Handout 4A: Poem Comparison

Directions: Analyze the two poems to understand how they each use language to inspire.

	"'Hope' is the thing with feathers—"	"Dreams"
What is the role of metaphor?		
What is the tone?	Tone: Evidence:	Tone: Evidence:
How does the structure impact the poem's meaning? (Consider stanzas or rhyme scheme.)	Structure description: Structure impact:	Structure description: Structure impact:
What is the impact of sound repetition on one stanza? (Consider rhyme or alliteration.)	Sound repetition example: Sound repetition impact:	Sound repetition example: Sound repetition impact:

	"'Hope' is the thing with feathers—"	"Dreams"
How does imagery impact the poem's meaning?	Imagery example (sketch or write): Image impact:	Imagery example (sketch or write): Image impact:
What is the theme/message?	Theme: Evidence:	Theme: Evidence:

Name

Date   Class

What are the most significant similarities and differences in how these poems use language to inspire?

_____

_____

_____

_____

_____

_____

_____

_____

_____

_____

_____

_____

_____

_____

_____

_____

_____

_____

_____

_____

_____

_____

_____

_____

_____

Name _____

Date _____ Class _____

Handout 5A: The Suffix -dom

Directions: In Part 1, predict the meaning of the suffix -dom based on your knowledge of the words and on the context of the sentences provided. Record the actual definition in Part 2. In Part 3, use the definition of -dom and the context sentences to define each word. Finally, in Part 4, make up a word ending in -dom to express the opposite of *freedom* and then use the newly created word in a sentence to explain how Maya Angelou's contrast between the concepts of being caged and free create deeper meaning in the poem.

Part 1

kingdom	The kingdom went on for miles, including both cities and rural areas.
boredom	With no toys or books, the child complained of boredom.
wisdom	The judge's decision showed great wisdom, as she found a solution fair to all.
fandom	The band had a small but devoted fandom consisting primarily of teenagers.
stardom	The actor achieved overnight stardom after performing in a top-grossing movie.
martyrdom	Followers of many religions have suffered martyrdom, as they have been killed for their beliefs.
queendom	The queen looked out of her castle window and surveyed her queendom.

Prediction of the meaning of the suffix –dom:

_____

_____

_____

Part 2

Word Part	Meaning
–dom (suffix)	

Part 3

kingdom _____

_____

boredom _____

_____

wisdom _____

_____

fandom _____

_____

stardom _____

_____

martyrdom _____

_____

queendom _____

_____

Part 4: Land

New word ending in *-dom* _____

Used in a sentence _____

_____

_____

Name _____

Date _____ Class _____

Handout 6A: Comic Strip Poetry

Directions: Draw a three-panel comic strip representing images from "Caged Bird." Caption each panel with a quotation and then analyze its language using a least one word from the word bank.

Analysis Word Bank: *figurative language, imagery, metaphor, stanza, alliteration, repetition, rhyme, speaker, juxtaposition*

Caption:

Analysis:

Caption:

Analysis:

Caption:

Analysis:

Name

Date   Class

Handout 7A: "Ask Not" Jigsaw

Directions: First, fill out your section of the handout. Then, after consulting with other "experts," share your information with your group and complete the rest of the handout.

Section	Central Idea	Supporting Details	What method(s) did Kennedy use to inspire in this section?
1: Paragraph 21		Detail 1: Detail 2:	
2: Paragraphs 22–23		Detail 1: Detail 2:	
3: Paragraph 24		Detail 1: Detail 2:	

Section	Central Idea	Supporting Details	What method(s) did Kennedy use to inspire in this section?
4: Paragraphs 25–26		Detail 1: Detail 2:	
5: Paragraph 27		Detail 1: Detail 2:	

When you return to your original group, summarize what this speech aims to inspire people to do.

Name _____

Date _____ Class _____

Handout 8A: Video Analysis

Directions: Record observations as you view the video. Then, analyze their effects.

	Observations: What specific details do you notice?	**Analysis:** How do these details affect the meaning of the speech?
Vocal Details (e.g., pausing after specific words, speed, volume, tone)		
Image Details (e.g., facial expressions, body language, setting, and people)		

Name

Date   Class

Handout 9A: Language Scavenger Hunt

Directions: In column 1, identify the type of language you are being asked to find. In column 2, record an example from "I Have a Dream." Then, when your teacher signals the hunt's end, write at least four analyses in column 3.

1. Item *Record what the sticky note says.*	2. Example *Record a quotation that includes an example.*	3. Analysis *How does this example affect the meaning of the speech?*

1. Item *Record what the sticky note says.*	2. Example *Record a quotation that includes an example.*	3. Analysis *How does this example affect the meaning of the speech?*

Name _____

Date _____ Class _____

Handout 9B: Concision Exercise

Directions: First, read the paragraph and annotate for concision. Remember to:

- Delete unnecessary words.
- Replace multiple words with single words (when possible).
- Avoid phrases like *there is* and *there are* (when possible).
- Replace prepositional phrases with adjectives or adverbs (when possible).

Concision in writing can be basically defined as "the quality of saying a whole lot in very few words." Concise writing is to the point, but it is not always short in length or low in word count. The important thing in concision is that the writer does not include any words or sentences that are unnecessary. Every word on the page has meaning and serves a purpose. Sometimes, writers will intentionally repeat or add words. They might do this to create rhythm, emphasize ideas, or achieve a specific style. For most of us, though, in most writing tasks or assignments or products, concise writing is a worthy goal to have to be sure our writing is meaningful and not wordy or redundant.

Revised Paragraph:

_____

_____

_____

_____

_____

_____

_____

Name

Date

Class

Handout 10A: Socratic Seminar Preparation

Directions: To prepare to discuss the most inspiring texts, analyze three effective techniques writers use to inspire. Your quotations can be from any of the poems or speeches.

Techniques	Quotations *Where do the writers and speakers use these techniques? (Cite!)*	Effects *How do these examples inspire an audience?*
Technique 1:		
Technique 2:		

Techniques	Quotations *Where do the writers and speakers use these techniques? (Cite!)*	Effects *How do these examples inspire an audience?*
Technique 3:		

Name _____

Date _____ Class _____

Handout 10B: Precision and Concision Review

Peer Reviewer:

Author of Paragraph Reviewed:

Directions: Use this checklist to evaluate your partner's Focusing Question Task 1 paragraph. Use a + if the writer has met the criterion. Use a Δ if you see a need for a change. Then, add notes to provide additional praise and/or suggestions.

Precision	+/△
▪ The nouns used are clear, specific, and appropriate to the content.	
Praise/Suggestions:	
▪ The verbs used are clear and exact.	
Praise/Suggestions:	
▪ The paragraph does not include imprecise words, such as *lots, a lot, things, many*, and so on.	
Praise/Suggestions:	

Concision	+/△
• Sentences do not contain unnecessary words.	
Praise/Suggestions:	
• The paragraph does not contain unnecessary sentences.	
Praise/Suggestions:	
• Repetition is used only for effect.	
Praise/Suggestions:	

Name _____

Date _____   Class _____

Handout 11A: Speaking and Listening Goal-Setting and Self-Assessment

Directions: Use this tool to set a goal for and assess your participation in the Socratic Seminar by marking + for *yes* and Δ for *needs improvement* in the appropriate boxes.

Before the Discussion: Set a Goal

My goal for this discussion is to:

_____

_____

_____

After the Discussion: Self-Assess

Criteria	+/ Δ
I came prepared for the discussion.	
I asked questions.	
I responded to questions.	
I made relevant observations.	
I acknowledged and elaborated on others' ideas.	
I listened carefully.	
I brought the discussion back on topic as needed.	
I agreed and disagreed respectfully.	
• I did not interrupt.	
• I used a polite tone of voice.	
• I disagreed with the statement, not the person.	
I used appropriate, formal, academic language. For example:	
I used vocabulary that I learned in this module, such as these words:	

I met my goal for this discussion.   YES / NO

Explain:

_____

_____

_____

My goal for the next discussion is to:

_____

_____

_____

Name _____

Date _____ Class _____

Handout 11B: Alternate and Opposing Claims

Directions: For each set of claims, decide whether the claims are alternate or opposing, and explain your thinking. Then, write the type of other claim that is missing. (If the claim is alternate, write an opposing claim, and vice versa.)

Set 1

Claim 1: Out of all the writers and speakers, Malala uses the technique of repetition most effectively to inspire.

Claim 2: In the poem "Caged Bird," Maya Angelou uses the technique of repetition most effectively to inspire.

Are these claims alternate or opposing? _____

Why?

_____

_____

_____

What would an alternate or opposing claim be?

_____

_____

Set 2

Claim 1: Of all the writers and speakers we studied, Langston Hughes's use of metaphor is the most effective in inspiring his audience.

Claim 2: Of all the writers and speakers we studied, Langston Hughes's use of metaphor is the least effective in inspiring his audience.

Are these claims alternate or opposing? _____

Why?

_____

_____

_____

What would an alternate or opposing claim be?

_____

_____

Name _____

Date _____ Class _____

Handout 12A: Word Comparison

Directions: Complete the Venn diagram by comparing how the acts of being persuasive and making an argument are similar and different. Write the ways that they are the same where the circles intersect. Write how each act is different in the appropriate circle.

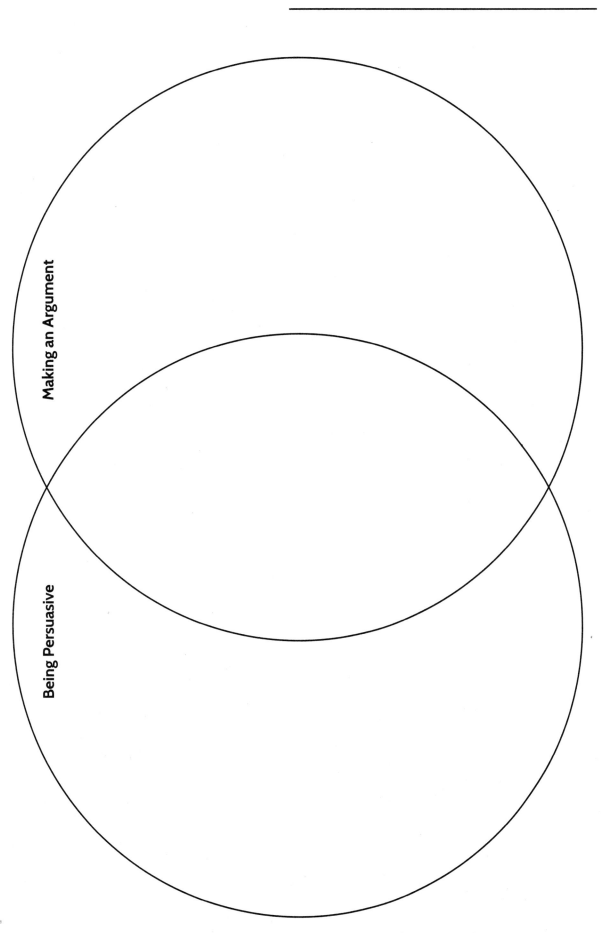

Making an Argument

Being Persuasive

Name _____

Date _____ Class _____

Handout 13A: Article Summary

Directions: Complete the chart with evidence from the article, "How Advertising Targets Our Children."

	Evidence from the Article
Products marketed to children:	
Effects on children of the advertising of these products:	
Strategies advertisers use to market these products to children:	
Factors that make children especially vulnerable to advertising:	

Name _____

Date _____ Class _____

Handout 14A: Argument Analysis

Directions: Complete the chart below, citing evidence from the article when appropriate.

What claim is the author making about advertising?	
What reason(s) does the author offer for her claim?	
What evidence does the author offer to support her reasons?	

Name _____

Date _____   Class _____

Handout 14B: The Three Appeals

Directions: Complete the chart by placing an X to identify which appeal(s) each ad is making. (Each ad might have more than one X.)

	Pathos: An appeal to emotion.	Logos: An appeal to logic or reason.	Ethos: An appeal to character or credibility.
"Serena Williams—Rise"			
Soda Ad I			
Soda Ad II			
Car Ad I			
Dessert Ad			
Car Ad II			

Reflect on and be ready to discuss what you notice about where the Xs are placed and what that reveals about advertising.

Name _____

Date _____   Class _____

Handout 14C: Advertising Techniques

Directions: Study the technique assigned to your group, and identify examples of that technique in a few of the ads we have studied. When other groups share, record their examples in the appropriate row on the chart.

Technique	Examples from the Ads We Studied
Misleading Words or Evidence: The ad appears to present facts or evidence, but those facts are either false or meaningless, or the ad omits key facts.	
Transfer: The ad tries to make consumers think of positive words or images when they think of the product.	
Plain Folks: The message the ad sends is that the product is popular with ordinary, trustworthy people like the viewer.	

Technique	Examples from the Ads We Studied
Bandwagon: The message is that everyone else is buying or using this product, so the people watching the ad better hurry and get on the bandwagon and buy the product themselves!	
Meaningless Slogan: The advertisement has a catchy phrase or slogan that is repeated many times and sticks with consumers.	
Celebrity Testimonial or Endorsement: A famous person or expert says she or he uses the product or recommends it.	

Name _____

Date _____ Class _____

Handout 14D: Functions of Phrases and Clauses

Directions: Brainstorm what you remember about phrases, independent clauses, and dependent clauses, and record your ideas in the first row of the table. Revise as needed after class discussion. When directed, identify whether the underlined examples in the paragraph are phrases, dependent clauses, or independent clauses, and note their function. When directed, return to the second row of the chart and record ideas about the purposes those phrases and clauses serve.

	Phrases	Independent Clauses	Dependent Clauses
What is it?			
Functions or purposes			

Argument Paragraph:

The ad "Rise" shows that an inspiring ad may not be as persuasive as other types of ads because the consumer may be left feeling

inspired but not persuaded to buy the product. Numerous elements combine to make "Rise" inspiring. The song is uplifting and catchy,

sticking with the viewer long after the ad ends. It also sends a musical message to keep fighting even when things are tough. The ad

designer also tells a compelling story, starting with how desolate Serena Williams feels at the beginning of the ad, as she gets up early

and remembers her negative press coverage and bad tennis moments. From that low point, though, the story "rises," as she begins

to run, especially when she begins running up the stairs. By the time she reaches the top of those stairs, she is remembering better

moments from her career, the times of great shots and winning trophies. The combination of the song and the story leave the viewer

feeling inspired to play tennis, run, or surmount other obstacles, but the question is … what is being advertised? It is hard to even

remember that part of the ad. The inspiring story and music would cause most viewers to overlook the product—a particular brand of

headphones. While the ad is powerful, it does not necessarily persuade viewers to buy headphones, which is, after all, the point.

Name

Date   Class

Handout 15A: Experiment with Phrases

Directions: Use carets and other needed editing marks to add phrases to the following paragraph to create transitions, add detail and precision, or clarify relationships.

When students improve their noticing and wondering skills, they become better readers. They pay closer attention

early. They think consciously about what questions they have. They develop a deeper understanding of what they read.

Many teachers report that students who notice and wonder well understand books at a deeper level. They demonstrate

this both through their work in class and high scores on reading assessments. One teacher pointed to her experience

with one student. She noticed only three basic facts and had no questions when her class read the first book of the year,

Castle Diary. This student struggled with comprehension early in the year. The year progressed. The student listened

to classmates share their observations and questions and received teacher support. She improved her noticing and

wondering skills. When the class read the first chapter of *Animal Farm*, the student listed over twenty important details,

including making connections to prior texts the class had read and recognizing the use of techniques such as figurative

language the class had learned about. The student wondered about many aspects of the book. She is a stronger reader

now. She demonstrates a solid understanding of *Animal Farm*. She makes astute comments in writing and in class

discussions. She performs well on New-Read Assessments and other assessments. Improving students' noticing and

wondering skills makes them more capable readers.

Name _____

Date _____   Class _____

Handout 16A: The Characters of *Animal Farm*

Directions: Use these character charts to keep track of who's who and of character developments as you read *Animal Farm*.

Character Chart 1: Old Major and the Pigs

Chapter	Description of the Character(s)	What's New, or How Has/Have the Character(s) Changed in this Chapter?

Character Chart 2: Napoleon

Chapter	Description of the Character(s)	What's New, or How Has/Have the Character(s) Changed in this Chapter?

Name

Date   Class

Character Chart 3: Snowball

Chapter	Description of the Character(s)	What's New, or How Has/Have the Character(s) Changed in this Chapter?

Character Chart 4: Squealer

Chapter	Description of the Character(s)	What's New, or How Has/Have the Character(s) Changed in this Chapter?

Name _____

Date _____ Class _____

Character Chart 5: Boxer

Chapter	Description of the Character(s)	What's New, or How Has/Have the Character(s) Changed in this Chapter?

Character Chart 6: Other Animals

Chapter	Description of the Character(s)	What's New, or How Has/Have the Character(s) Changed in this Chapter?

Name

Date   Class

Handout 16B: Excerpts from "Friedrich Engels, Revolutionary, Activist, Unionist, and Social Investigator"

Directions: Read the following excerpts to learn about Friedrich Engels, Karl Marx, and *The Communist Manifesto*.

Excerpts from "Friedrich Engels, Revolutionary, Activist, Unionist, and Social Investigator," Rosalie Baker

1   The phrase "workers of the world unite" was used by Karl Marx and Friedrich Engels to end their influential political work titled *The Communist Manifesto*. The *Manifesto* was a criticism of the state of factory workers during the dawn of the Industrial Revolution in Europe and a call to arms meant to inspire workers to fight for their rights. This one phrase has been used as the tagline for communist leaders since its initial publication in 1848…

2   Friedrich Engels was the oldest son of a German businessman who owned several factories. As a young man, Engels had a variety of interests, including reading "radical" literature that criticized the treatment of factory workers. During the Industrial Revolution, many factory owners made a great deal of money, but they did not share this new wealth with the workers. Factory employees also had to work very long hours, often in difficult conditions. It was these conditions that upset the young Friedrich Engels.

3   Engels knew about life in a factory. He had walked through streets polluted by factory emissions on his way to school. He also observed the living conditions of the city's working class, which he described as being worse than those of animals.…

* * *

4   The work of Karl Marx and Friedrich Engels not only introduced the world to communism and a classless society, it forced individuals to examine the capitalist system and inspired important historical events such as the Russian Revolution and the Cold War.

But There's Also Karl Marx

5   A German philosopher, political theorist, and revolutionary, Karl Marx is best known for the key role he played in the development of communism, a political and economic system in which property and resources are owned or controlled by the public or the state. His basic belief that history is a constant struggle between the rich and the poor is stated in the opening sentence of *The Communist Manifesto*.

Baker, Rosalie. "Friedrich Engels, Revolutionary, Activist, Unionist, and Social Investigator." *Calliope*, 30 People Who Changed the World. *Cricket Media*, Carus Publishing Company.

Name

Date   Class

Handout 16C: Key Terms, Events, People, and Places

Directions: Read the following to learn key terms, events, people, and places helpful to understanding the allegorical nature of *Animal Farm*.

Term	Definitions, Descriptions, and Examples
capitalism	An economic system in which individuals, not the government, own property and businesses.
communism	"[A] political and economic system in which property and resources are owned or controlled by the public or the state." Excerpts from "Friedrich Engels, Revolutionary, Activist, Unionist, and Social Investigator," Rosalie Baker (Handout 16B) An economic system in which the government, not individuals, owns property and businesses.
class	A group of people who all share similar economic circumstances or social rank or standing.
economic	Having to do with the making, buying, and selling of goods and the provision, buying, and selling of services.
working class	The label given to a class or group of people who work for wages, usually by working in a factory or doing manual, or physical, labor.
Russian Revolution of 1917	A revolt, taking place over several years, during which a group of rebels, led by Vladimir Lenin, ultimately overthrew and took over the Russian government. Before the revolution, Russia had a Tsar who was a monarch or king and who exercised a great deal of power over the people. The revolutionaries rebelled because of what they saw as the unfairness and injustice of the system and because they believed that under that system, those in the upper classes were taking advantage of working people and others in the lower classes. The leaders of the movement embraced the general theories of Karl Marx and Friedrich Engels and established a new political and economic system based on those. They labeled their new political and economic system communism.
Vladimir Lenin	A leader of the Russian communist revolutionary movement that overthrew the Russian tsar. Lenin was the first leader of the Soviet Union, serving from 1917 until his death in 1924.
Soviet Union	The name given to the new country formed when revolutionaries adhering to communism overthrew the Russian government. The Soviet Union lasted from 1917 until it was disbanded in 1992.
Joseph Stalin	The Russian revolutionary who ruled the Soviet Union from the time of Lenin's death in 1924 until his own death in 1953.

Name _____

Date _____   Class _____

Handout 16D: Experiment with Clauses

Directions: In the space provided below, write a portion of an argument paragraph using the claim, reasons, and evidence in the following table. As you write, use at least two clauses to make transitions or clarify the relationship among the claim, reasons, and evidence in the paragraph. Underline the clauses used.

Claim	Old Major is the most respected animal on the farm.
Reasons	All the animals admire him, want to hear what he says, and are moved by his speech.
Evidence	<ul><li>"[T]here was a stirring and a fluttering all through the farm buildings" because "[w]ord had gone round during the day" (3) that Old Major was going to speak about his strange dream.</li><li>"Old Major was so highly regarded on the farm that everyone was quite willing to lose an hour's sleep to hear what he had to say." (4)</li><li>When he calls for a vote as to whether rats are comrades, an overwhelming majority agrees that they are, based on what he has said. (10)</li><li>All the animals join in the singing of his song. (13)</li><li>His speech is quite long, but there is no mention of any restlessness, so a reader could infer that the other animals respect him and are listening to him.</li></ul>

Revision with Clauses:

_____

_____

_____

_____

_____

_____

_____

_____

_____

_____

Name

Date   Class

Handout 17A: Techniques of Persuasion

Directions: For each technique of persuasion, list one (or more) examples from Old Major's speech and song.

A few rows have been done for you as examples.

Techniques of Persuasion in Old Major's Speech and Song, *Animal Farm*, Chapter I	
Technique	Example
1. Engage Your Audience When an audience is interested, they are more likely to be persuaded. Do this by: • Using an introduction that makes them want to learn more. • Posing rhetorical questions, or questions that do not require an answer and are asked to encourage the audience to think about the issue. • Use inclusive language, words like *we* and *us*. • Connect by referring to your audience directly or by name.	Make Them Want to Hear More: ▪ *Old Major says, "But I will come to the dream later on" (6). Since his audience came to hear about his dream, they will stay until he tells about the dream.*
	Ask Rhetorical Questions:
	Use Inclusive Language:
	Connect:

Techniques of Persuasion in Old Major's Speech and Song, *Animal Farm*, Chapter I	
Technique	Example
2. Compliment Your Audience When you flatter others, they are more likely to be persuaded.	
3. Create a Sense of Urgency When something seems urgent ("This offer is good for today only!"), it is more persuasive.	
4. Inspire Your Audience Give your audience a vision of how their lives could be if they believed or acted as you are telling them to do.	
5. Use the Power of Images Creating images in someone's mind helps to persuade them.	

Name _____

Date _____ Class _____

Techniques of Persuasion in Old Major's Speech and Song, *Animal Farm*, Chapter I	
Technique	Example
6. Convince the Audience that You Have Authority When the audience believes in you, they are more likely to believe in your ideas. Do this by: ▪ Establishing your authority. ▪ Using words that sound fair and unbiased. ▪ Using correct grammar and formal language.	Authority: Fair, Unbiased Words: Correct Grammar and Formal Language:

Techniques of Persuasion in Old Major's Speech and Song, *Animal Farm*, Chapter I	
Technique	Example
7. Appeal to Your Audience's Emotions When the audience feels something, they are more likely to believe something. Do this by: • Making your audience feel strongly (an emotion like anger, for example). • Telling stories of emotional events. • Using emotional words and phrases (think about connotation and not just denotation).	Inspiring Emotion:
	Emotional Stories:
	Emotional Words and Phrases: • *Old Major does not just say they will be killed; he says they will be "slaughtered with hideous cruelty" (7).*
8. Convince Your Audience with Logic and Reason When the audience thinks that something is true, they are more likely to believe it. Do this by: • Citing facts and statistics. • Constructing logical arguments (if this is true, then that must be true).	Facts and Statistics:
	Logical Arguments:

Name _____

Date _____ Class _____

Techniques of Persuasion in Old Major's Speech and Song, *Animal Farm*, Chapter I	
Technique	Example
9. Address Objections Explaining why alternate or opposing arguments are wrong helps convince your audience.	▪ *Old Major warns them not to listen to anyone else or think about other ideas. For example, he says never to listen to Man: "It is all lies" (10).*
10. Repeat Ideas Repeating ideas helps reinforce your message.	
11. Use Mottos and Simple Phrases Reducing complex ideas to simple words and phrases helps ensure that everyone understands and remembers your argument.	▪ *Old Major says, "Whatever goes upon two legs is an enemy" (11).*
12. Create an Enemy Creating an us-versus-them feeling helps convince others to side with you.	

Name _____

Date _____ Class _____

Handout 18A: The Seven Commandments

Directions: Use this handout to think about the animals' seven commandments and what the text says or what you infer about why they included each one.

	Commandment	Evidence or Inferences about Why the Pigs Included this Commandment
1	Whatever goes upon two legs is an enemy.	
2	Whatever goes upon four legs, or has wings, is a friend.	
3	No animal shall wear clothes.	

	Commandment	Evidence or Inferences about Why the Pigs Included this Commandment
4	No animal shall sleep in a bed.	
5	No animal shall drink alcohol.	
6	No animal shall kill any other animal.	
7	All animals are equal.	

Name _____

Date _____   Class _____

Handout 19A: Comparison of Characters' Perspectives

Directions: Complete the Venn diagram by comparing and contrasting Napoleon and Snowball's perspectives on the events that have taken place so far on Animal Farm. Write the ways that their perspectives are the same where the circles intersect. Write each character's differing perspectives in that character's circle.

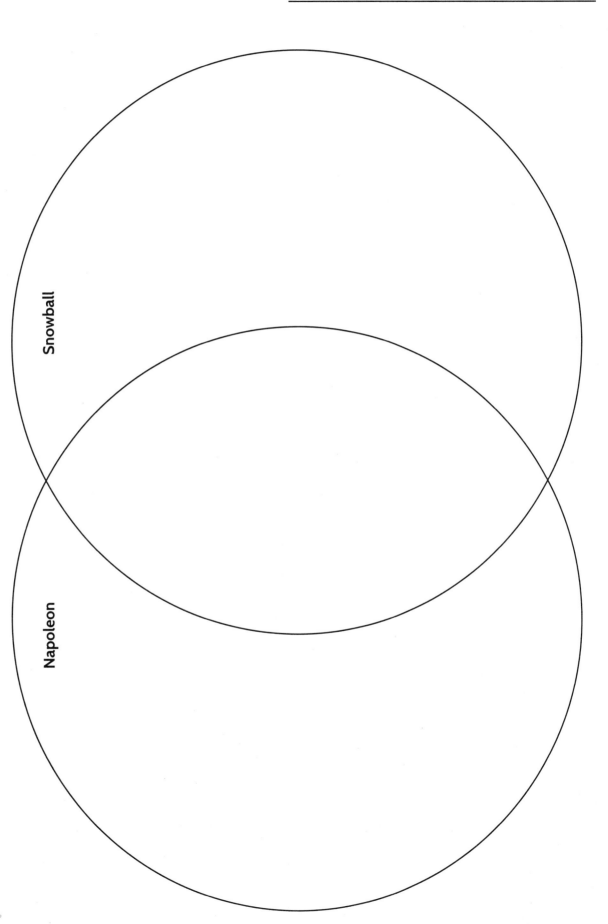

Snowball

Napoleon

Name _____

Date _____ Class _____

Handout 19B: Analysis of Squealer's Milk-and-Apples Argument

Directions: Fill in the table during the class discussion. Then answer the questions that follow. Note: Squealer's argument occurs at the end of chapter III, on pages 35–36.

Claim	
Reason(s)	
Evidence	

1. Are his reasons sound? Do they support his claim? Explain.

_____

_____

_____

_____

_____

2. Is his evidence accurate, relevant, and sufficient? Explain.

_____

_____

_____

_____

_____

3. Look at this list of persuasive techniques we have discussed. Which does Squealer use? (Circle the ones he uses, and jot your evidence.)

- Engage your audience.

- Compliment your audience.

- Create a sense of urgency.

- Inspire your audience.

- Use the power of images.

- Convince the audience that you have authority.

- Appeal to your audience's emotions.

- Convince your audience with logic and reason.

- Address objections.

- Repeat ideas.

- Use mottos and simple phrases.

- Create an enemy.

Name _____

Date _____ Class _____

4. Squealer anticipates that the other animals may have their own opposing argument when he says, "'Comrades! You do not imagine, I hope, that we pigs are doing this in a spirit of selfishness and privilege?'" (35) How does he address this opposing argument? Is he convincing?

_____

_____

_____

_____

_____

5. Who gains from his argument? Who suffers?

_____

_____

_____

6. Squealer gives reasons and evidence and addresses an opposing argument. Is his argument a strong one? Explain.

_____

_____

_____

_____

_____

_____

_____

_____

_____

Name _____

Date _____ Class _____

Handout 22A: Focusing Question Task 2 Review

Directions: Annotate and use these questions to review your own or a classmate's Focusing Question Task 2 response.

Writer:	Reviewer:

Claim Statement: Underline the claim.

Does the claim statement clearly state which of the animals was most influential in helping Napoleon gain power over the other animals?   YES / NO
If NO, how can it be improved?

Reasoning and Evidence: Underline the reasons given to support the claim, and place a check mark (☑) next to each piece of evidence.

Do the reasons and evidence logically support the claim?   YES / NO
If NO, how can the reasoning be more clearly explained?

Is the evidence relevant?   YES / NO
If NO, what evidence should be taken out?

Elaboration: Write a plus sign (+) to mark elaboration.

Does the paragraph include elaboration?   YES / NO
If NO, what should be added to clarify or explain the connection between the claim, reasons, and evidence?

Concluding Statement: Underline the concluding statement.

Does the concluding statement follow from and support the argument?   YES / NO
If NO, how can it be improved?

Cohesion

Does the paragraph demonstrate:

_____ A logical organization?

_____ Transitions that connect ideas and show how they relate to each other?

Notes:

Language and Style

Does the writer use:

_____ Precise language?

_____ Concise language, communicating his or her position as succinctly as possible?

_____ A formal style appropriate to purpose and audience?

Notes:

Conventions of Writing

Does the writer:

_____ Spell correctly?

_____ Punctuate correctly?

_____ Use correct grammar and sentence structures?

Notes:

Name

Date   Class

Handout 22B: Changes to the Seven Commandments of *Animal Farm*

Directions: Mark changes to the commandments in the first column. Write what the change means or reveals in the second column.

The Commandments	What the Change Means or Reveals
1. Whatever goes upon two legs is an enemy.	
2. Whatever goes upon four legs, or has wings, is a friend.	
3. No animal shall wear clothes.	

The Commandments	What the Change Means or Reveals
4. No animal shall sleep in a bed.	
5. No animal shall drink alcohol.	
6. No animal shall kill any other animal.	
7. All animals are equal.	

Name

Date   Class

Handout 25A: The Temples at Abu Simbel

Directions: Read the following excerpts from two articles to learn about Abu Simbel.

Excerpts from "Let's Tour the Temple"
by Ramadan B. Hussein

1   One of the most stunning monuments ever crafted in the ancient world is the Great Temple of Abu Simbel. It was built in Nubia for Ramesses II, ruler of Egypt from about 1290 B.C. to about 1224 B.C. Carving the massive structure into the slope of a mountain began in year four of Ramesses' reign and took around 20 years to complete.

2   For Ramesses, the monument was not only a testament to his country's might and technological superiority, but also a way to promote Egyptian religious beliefs. Amazingly, this temple remains essentially in its original form. Nature itself protected it, as through the centuries, wind-blown sand gradually covered the entrance.

Beloved of Amun

3   Known today as the Great Temple of Abu Simbel, it was called "Temple of Ramesses, beloved of Amun" by the ancients. The Egyptians had conquered Nubia, the territory that lay to the south, and so, to promote loyalty to himself and to Egypt, Ramesses encouraged his Nubian subjects to worship him as a god. At the time, Egyptians throughout the country honored three gods as state or national deities:

Ptah, the principal deity of the city of Memphis, the ancient capital of Egypt; Re-Horakhty, a form of the sun god worshiped in Heliopolis, an important religious center; and Amun, the creator god of Thebes, the capital of Egypt....

Art as Propaganda

4   The scenes depicted on the walls show the king in battle against the Hittites, Libyans, and Nubians. While all represent actual campaigns that took place during Ramesses' reign, the most important was the Battle of Kadesh, in what is present-day Syria. There Egyptian forces clashed with the Hittites of Anatolia (present-day Turkey).

5   Both states had powerful armies, and each wanted control of the land that lay between them. Known as the Levant, it includes the present-day countries of Syria, Lebanon, and Israel. The armies met in Kadesh, along the Orontes River. Tricked into believing that the Hittites were farther away than they were, Ramesses chose to divide his forces as part of his plan of attack. Fortunately for Ramesses, the rest of his troops arrived in time to help him after he had been ambushed.

6   According to the scenes on monuments erected by Ramesses, it was a total victory for the Egyptian forces. In the text, he even bragged that, at one point, he had fought his way through the Hittites singlehandedly. The actual events, however, were probably not as one-sided as he claimed. Nevertheless, the battle did result in the two empires agreeing on a fixed border between them and drafting what is the world's first known peace treaty. In it, the empires agreed to become allies and to aid each other in future wars. To further ensure good relations between the Egyptians and Hittites, Ramesses married a Hittite princess...

Perfection in Design

7   The temple was designed with such precision that the statues at the back of the temple are in perfect alignment with the outermost entrance. This means that light from outside can shine through the entrance to the figures along the back wall—to all, that is, except Ptah. The Egyptians honored Ptah as the sun at night and thus positioned his figure to remain always in darkness. Twice each year, on February 20 and October 20, the first rays of the rising sun shine directly into the sanctuary. It is believed—but the proof is still not conclusive—that these calendar dates were significant. They may have been Ramesses' birthday and coronation day.

Citation: Hussein, Ramadan B. "Let's Tour the Temple." *Dig*, Oct. 2010. Cricket Media, Carus Publishing Company.

Name _____

Date _____ Class _____

Excerpts from "Grandeur at Abu Simbel"
by Steven Snape

1   Of these temples [commissioned by Ramesses II], the greatest was Abu Simbel. It was located at Aswan, 170 miles south of the ancient southern boundary of Egypt. No trace of any sort of ancient town or settlement has been uncovered, even though Abu Simbel lies in one of the most populated parts of Nubia, and archaeologists assume there must have been one.

2   The site was known to kings of the 18th Dynasty, and a small temple belonging to King Horemheb has been uncovered nearby. However, it was only under Ramesses II that Abu Simbel was established as the most magnificent of the Nubian temples.

3   There are actually two buildings at Abu Simbel. The Great Temple is dedicated to four important Egyptian gods: the falcon-headed sun god Ra-Harakhty; Amun-Re, god of Thebes and protector of the Egyptian empire; Ptah, god of Memphis, the largest city in Egypt; and Ramesses himself. In fact, Ramesses planned all of his major Nubian temples with the intention of promoting himself as a god in his own lifetime. The ancient name of what is today called the Great Temple was "The House of Ramesses, beloved of Amun."

4   Because of the difficulties involved in cutting into rock, the interior of the Great Temple is comparatively small, and the carvings on the walls are not especially remarkable. They feature the traditional scenes of the king making offerings to the gods, but among them are some rather strange images of Ramesses, the living king, making offerings to himself, the god. The military victories of which Ramesses was so proud are also heavily featured, especially the battle of Kadesh (see pages 4–7). Other scenes emphasize his military might by depicting him subduing both the Libyans and the local Nubians. The temple also features inscriptions that detail important events later in Ramesses' reign, including a rock-cut stele describing his marriage to a Hittite princess in the 34th year of his reign.

5   The Small Temple is dedicated to a local version of the sky goddess Hathor and also features Queen Nefertari, accompanied by symbols of the traits that identified her as the personification of Hathor.

6   The façades of both are justly famous. From a great distance, the viewer can see that four colossal seated statues of Ramesses dominate the front of the larger structure. Each is 65 feet tall. The standing figures of Nefertari and her husband on the façade of the Small Temple are each about 33 feet tall. The Great Temple also shows some of the most important members of Ramesses' family, but all are very small figures standing alongside his ankles.

7   So, although the inner workings of an Egyptian temple would be hidden from, and mysterious to, an outsider, the external appearance of these mighty buildings would be a clear message to Nubians that their king, living in distant Pi-Ramesses, Thebes, or Memphis, was to be feared and worshiped as a living god....

Citation: Snape, Steven. "Grandeur at Abu Simel." *Calliope*, Oct. 2005. Cricket Media, Carus Publishing Company.

Name _____

Date _____ Class _____

Handout 26A: Two Arguments

Directions: Read these two arguments to reflect on the source of Stalin's power and the structure of an effective argument.

Argument 1: Real-Life Proof of the Power of Language

1   The most evil dictator of all time? Although today he is remembered as ruling by fear and threats, in his lifetime Stalin created an image for himself as a man of the people and a champion of the workers. By rewriting truth and creating propaganda, Joseph Stalin used language to gain and maintain power. He did so in a number of ways.

2   By rewriting the truth, Stalin changed the "facts" so they supported him. He changed his name to Stalin, which means "the man of steel." He had history books rewritten, to tell more positive stories of his part in the Russian Revolution. To delete evidence of those who he had killed, Stalin had his officials alter records to remove names. When people who worked for him fell out of favor, Stalin had photographs altered to remove the person from the picture. People who doubted Stalin might have had a hard time finding evidence against him. By changing "facts," Stalin was able to convince people that the "truth" was that he was a strong hero without enemies.

3   In addition, Stalin was masterful at using visual images to communicate ideas. He used propaganda posters with pictures of him with common people and babies. He made other posters showing pig faces for the farmers who resisted him. By showing himself as kind and caring, and his enemies as pigs, Stalin created a positive image of himself. His use of visuals helped consolidate his power.

4   With words and images, Stalin created a cult of personality around himself. He called himself Comrade Stalin, a "friend" to the people. He made his name part of the country's national anthem. His image made it easier for people to see him as a great leader, without thinking critically about his policies. One could argue that his greatest power was in his cruel actions. He had countless people killed, but how did he get away with murder? He used language and pictures to show himself as a hero and a friend.

5   Stalin led the Soviet Union from 1929 to 1953. Under his rule the country transformed from a country of farmers to an industrial superpower. Although he ruled by fear and total control, because of his brilliant control of language and propaganda, he was remembered by many in his country as a great leader.

Argument 2: Stalin's Brutal Reign

1 He helped to defeat the Nazis. He made the Soviet Union a world superpower. What he is most remembered for, though, is his reign of terror. Although his image as a Soviet hero may have convinced some, fear and violence were the most essential elements of Stalin's dictatorship. He showed himself to be a ruthless leader time and time again.

2 Even when farmers resisted and people were starving, Stalin continued with his plans. To create a communist state, Stalin decided to combine small, peasant-owned farms into state-run farms. When small farmers resisted, they were arrested and then killed or sent away. The new farms did not produce enough food, and the food they did produce was used to feed those in the cities or exported for sale. Many who had grown the food then had no food to eat themselves. Some estimate that five to ten million people starved to death under this plan.

3 When people stood in his way, Stalin thought nothing of having them killed. Instead of trying to work with people who disagreed with him, Stalin instituted the Great Purge, which was a plan to get rid of any people he considered a threat to himself, the Communist Party, or the Soviet Union. He had fake, show trials of his enemies, many who falsely confessed and were sentenced to death and executed. He created scapegoats so people would have someone else to blame for problems and could come together against a shared enemy. Knowing how he treated his enemies would have made it difficult to resist Stalin!

4 To be sure, Stalin used other techniques to cement his position. He controlled the media and the press. He knew how to manipulate people and negotiate to get what he wanted. He used propaganda to show himself in a positive way. None of this would have mattered, though, if he had not also been willing to kill his enemies and let his citizens die.

5 No one knows exactly how many died under Stalin's reign of terror, but some estimate that his decisions and orders led to the deaths of twenty million people. He did not protect individuals' security or help their well-being. Instead, he ruthlessly made every decision with one goal: to create a world power. In this he succeeded, but at such a high cost that he is remembered as one of the most evil dictators in history.

Name

Date

Class

Works Cited

BBC Staff. "Joseph Stalin: National Hero or Cold-Blooded Murderer?" *BBC: iWonder*, Web. Accessed 15 Sept. 2016.

Hingley, Ronald Francis. "Joseph Stalin." *Encyclopædia Britannica*. Encyclopædia Britannica Online, Encyclopædia Britannica, 23 Nov. 2015, Web. Accessed 15 Sept. 2016.

History.com Staff. "Joseph Stalin." *History.com*. A&E Networks, 2009. **www.history.com/topics/joseph-stalin**. Accessed 20 Aug. 2016.

McCollum, Sean. *Joseph Stalin*. A Wicked History, Scholastic, 2010.

Name _____

Date _____ Class _____

Handout 26B: Allegory in *Animal Farm*

Directions: Use the chart to map the parallels between *Animal Farm* and the rise of Stalin in the Soviet Union.

	Stalin and the Soviet Union	Animal Farm
Who is overthrown to form the new society?		
Who becomes the supreme leader?		
How does the supreme leader prevent people from disagreeing?		
What was the political philosophy that was the basis for the revolution?		
Into what two groups is society divided?		

Why would *Animal Farm* be described as an allegory?

_____

_____

_____

_____

Name _____

Date _____ Class _____

Handout 27A: The Ideal vs. the Reality

Directions: Use this handout to reflect on and record ideas about life on the animals' farm. The first example in each row has been done for you.

What are the signs of a growing class divide on the farm?	▪ *The rations for most of the animals, except the pigs and dogs, are reduced.*
What does this mean for the pigs? **For the other animals?**	▪ *The pigs are getting fatter, while the other animals are hungry.*
How do the pigs try to hide or gloss over what they are doing?	▪ *They use words to try to hide what is actually happening. Squealer says they had to adjust the rations: "Squealer always spoke of it as a 'readjustment,' never as a 'reduction'" (112).*

Name _____

Date _____   Class _____

Handout 28A: The Final Commandment

Directions: Add the final commandment. Then compare the original commandments to the final one and reflect on the significance.

Original Commandments:

Final Commandment:

_____

_____

_____

_____

_____

1. Whatever goes upon two legs is an enemy.

2. Whatever goes upon four legs, or has wings, is a friend.

3. No animal shall wear clothes.

4. No animal shall sleep in a bed.

5. No animal shall drink alcohol.

6. No animal shall kill any other animal.

7. All animals are equal.

Compare the original seven commandments with the final one commandment. What does this show about the animals' farm?

_____

_____

_____

_____

_____

_____

_____

Name _____

Date _____ Class _____

Handout 29A: Speaking and Listening Goal-Setting and Self-Assessment

Directions: Use this tool to set a goal for and assess your participation in the Socratic Seminar by marking + for *yes* and Δ for *needs improvement* in the appropriate boxes.

Before the Discussion: Set a Goal

My goal for this discussion is to:

_____

_____

_____

After the Discussion: Self-Assess

Criteria	+/ △
I came prepared for the discussion.	
I posed questions.	
I responded to questions.	
I made relevant observations.	
I acknowledged and elaborated on others' ideas.	
I listened carefully.	
I brought the discussion back on topic as needed.	
I agreed and disagreed respectfully.	
• I did not interrupt.	
• I used a polite tone of voice.	
• I disagreed with the statement, not the person.	
I used appropriate, formal, academic language. For example:	
I used vocabulary that I learned in this module, such as these words:	
Total number of **+**'s	

I met my goal for this discussion.   YES   /   NO

Explain:

_____

_____

_____

My goal for the next discussion is to:

_____

_____

_____

Name _____

Date _____ Class _____

Handout 29B: Focusing Question Task 3 Evidence Organizer

Directions: Use this tool to reflect on the Socratic Seminar and prepare for Focusing Question Task 3. Complete the top two rows first. Identify three central ideas or themes that Orwell develops about the power of language in *Animal Farm* and provide textual evidence for each.

Central Ideas and Themes in Orwell's *Animal Farm*		
Central Idea or Theme:	Central Idea or Theme:	Central Idea or Theme:
Evidence:	Evidence:	Evidence:

Name _____

Date _____ Class _____

Handout 30A: Argument Outline

Directions: Review the Focusing Question Task 3 prompt and checklist for success. Then, complete the organizer to plan a response.

Claim:

| |
| |

Reasons:

1:	2:
Evidence: 1. 2.	**Evidence:** 1. 2.

Alternate or Opposing Claim:

| |
| |

Concluding Statement:

| |
| |

Name _____

Date _____ Class _____

Handout 31A: *New Republic* Jigsaw

Directions: Identify how Soule supports his position on *Animal Farm* in each paragraph.

	Central Ideas **(How do your two paragraphs convey Soule's position on *Animal Farm*?)**
1. Paragraphs 1–2	
2. Paragraphs 3–4	
3. Paragraphs 5–6	
4. Paragraphs 7–8	
5. Paragraphs 9–10	

Write a one-sentence summary that expresses Soule's position on *Animal Farm*:

_____

_____

Name _____

Date _____ Class _____

Handout 31B: *Animal Farm* Review Comparison

Directions: Use bullet points to jot notes comparing and contrasting the authors' positions on *Animal Farm*.

	New Republic Review	Teen Ink Review	Common Sense Media Review
Summarize the author's position on *Animal Farm*.			
What reasons does the author provide? (Give two or three reasons.)			

New Republic Review	Teen Ink Review	Common Sense Media Review
What evidence does the author provide? (Give two or three key details.)		

What are the most significant similarities and differences between these authors' portrayals of *Animal Farm*?

Name _____

Date _____ Class _____

Handout 33A: Argument Essay Checklist

Directions: Use this checklist to evaluate the draft. Mark a **+** to indicate that the writer has met the criterion. Mark a **Δ** to indicate the need for a change.

	Self +/△	Peer +/△	Teacher +/△
Structure			
I respond to all parts of the prompt.			
My claim is debatable, and I focus on it throughout the piece.			
I introduce the claim clearly in my introduction paragraph.			
I recognize and acknowledge an alternate or opposing claim.			
I organize my reasons and evidence clearly in body paragraphs.			
My conclusion paragraph supports the focus.			
I use transitions to smoothly and logically connect paragraphs and claims, reasons, and evidence.			
Development			
I support my claim with clear, logical reasons.			
I develop my claim with accurate evidence from the text(s).			
My evidence is relevant to the reasons I offer.			
I elaborate upon the evidence.			
Style and Conventions			
I use a variety of sentence patterns (simple, compound, complex, compound–complex) to add interest and signal differing relationships among ideas.			
I use vocabulary words that are specific and appropriate to the content.			
I write precisely and concisely, without using unnecessary words.			
I write in an appropriately formal style.			
My writing style is appropriate for the audience.			
Total number of +'s			

To Be Completed by the Peer Reviewer

Peer Reviewer Name: _____

Praise: _____

_____

_____

_____

_____

_____

Suggestion: _____

_____

_____

_____

_____

_____

_____

Name _____

Date _____ Class _____

Handout 34A: Argument Essay Evidence

Directions: Is language more powerful when used to uplift or to control? Before responding, gather evidence from both sides. Then you will weigh the evidence and determine the most accurate evidence-based claim.

	Claim 1: Language is more powerful when used to uplift.
Evidence from Animal Farm (Provide at least three examples.)	Evidence that supports Claim 1:
Evidence From One Other Text (Or Set of Texts) (Provide at least three examples.)	Evidence that supports Claim 1:

Claim 2: Language is more powerful when used to control.	
Evidence from *Animal Farm* (Provide at least three examples.)	Evidence that supports Claim 2:
Evidence From One Other Text (Or Set of Texts) (Provide at least three examples.)	Evidence that supports Claim 2:

Name _____

Date _____ Class _____

Handout 34B: Argument Essay Outline

Directions: Now that you have evaluated the evidence, outline your essay.

Claim:

Reasons:

1:

2:

Evidence:

1.

2.

Evidence:

1.

2.

Alternate or Opposing Claim:

What is one alternate or opposing claim readers could make, and what text-based reason might they provide?

What evidence could you use in response to this alternate or opposing claim?

Name _____

Date _____ Class _____

Handout 36A: Argument Essay Checklist

Directions: Use this checklist to evaluate the draft. Mark a + to indicate that the writer has met the criterion. Mark a △ to indicate the need for a change.

	Self +/△	Peer +/△	Teacher +/△
Reading Comprehension			
I demonstrate understanding of the relationship between language and power in *Animal Farm*.			
I demonstrate understanding of the relationship between language and power in one other text (or set of texts).			
Structure			
I respond to all parts of the prompt.			
My claim is debatable, and I focus on it throughout the piece.			
I introduce the claim clearly in my introduction paragraph.			
I recognize and acknowledge an alternate or opposing claim.			
I organize my reasons and evidence clearly in body paragraphs.			
My conclusion paragraph supports the focus.			
I use transitions to smoothly and logically connect paragraphs and claims, reasons, and evidence.			
Development			
I support my claim with clear, logical reasons.			
I develop my claim with accurate evidence from the text(s).			
My evidence is relevant to the reasons I offer.			
I elaborate upon the evidence.			
Style and Conventions			
I use a variety of sentence patterns (simple, compound, complex, compound-complex) to add interest and signal differing relationships among ideas.			
I use vocabulary words that are specific and appropriate to the content.			
I write precisely and concisely, without using unnecessary words.			

Style and Conventions	Self +/△	Peer +/△	Teacher +/△
I write in an appropriately formal style.			
My writing style is appropriate for the audience.			
Total number of +'s			

To Be Completed by the Peer Reviewer

Peer Reviewer Name: _____

Praise: _____

Suggestion: _____

_____

_____

_____

_____

Name _____

Date _____ Class _____

Handout 37A: Speaking and Listening Goal-Setting and Self-Assessment

Directions: Use this tool to set a goal for and assess your participation in the Socratic Seminar by marking + for *yes* and Δ for *needs improvement* in the appropriate boxes.

Before the Discussion: Set a Goal

My goal for this discussion is to:

_____

_____

_____

After the Discussion: Self-Assess

Criteria	+/Δ
I came prepared for the discussion.	
I posed questions.	
I responded to questions.	
I made relevant observations.	
I acknowledged and built on others' ideas.	
I listened carefully.	
I brought the discussion back on topic as needed.	
I agreed and disagreed respectfully.	
▪ I did not interrupt.	
▪ I used a polite tone of voice.	
▪ I disagreed with the statement, not the person.	
I used appropriate, formal, academic language. For example:	
I used vocabulary that I learned in this module, such as these words:	
Total number of **+**'s	

I met my goal for this discussion.   YES   /   NO

Explain:

_____

_____

_____

My goal for the next discussion is to:

_____

_____

_____

Volume of Reading Reflection Questions

Language and Power, Grade 7, Module 3

Student Name: _____

Text: _____

Author: _____

Topic: _____

_____

Genre/Type of Book: _____

Share your knowledge about language and power by answering the questions below.

Informational Texts

1. **Wonder:** What drew you to read this informational text? Cite three things you noticed or wondered as you first perused the book.

2. **Organize:** Summarize a central idea of the text and its development, including relevant details.

3. **Reveal:** Choose a part of the text that was particularly intriguing or powerful. Explain how the author used language to keep you interested as you read.

4. **Distill:** What is the most important insight you gained from this text? How does the insight relate to power?

5. **Know:** How does this text's emphasis on or interpretation of information add to or contrast with what you already know about this topic?

6. **Vocabulary:** Write and define three powerful vocabulary words that you learned in this text. Why is each word important to know in discussions where someone might use language to argue a point?

Literary Texts

1. **Wonder:** After reading the first few pages of the text, what inferences can you draw? Support the inferences with textual evidence.

2. **Organize:** Write a short, objective summary of the story including the main character(s), setting, conflict, and resolution.

3. **Reveal:** Choose two characters with different points of view and explain the contrast between them. Cite evidence for each.

4. **Distill:** What is a theme of this story? How does it develop over the course of the text?

5. **Know**: How does this text further your understanding of the use of language? Support your response with details from this text.

6. **Vocabulary:** Identify three words that you learned in this text that are key to understanding the role of language in persuading, inspiring, or displaying power. Explain each word's role in the effect.

WIT & WISDOM PARENT TIP SHEET

WHAT IS MY GRADE 7 STUDENT LEARNING IN MODULE 3?

Wit & Wisdom is our English curriculum. It builds knowledge of key topics in history, science, and literature through the study of excellent texts. By reading and responding to stories and nonfiction texts, we will build knowledge of the following topics:

Module 1: Identity in the Middle Ages

Module 2: Americans All

Module 3: Language and Power

Module 4: Fever

In the third module, *Language and Power*, students have many rich and engaging opportunities to explore the power of language to inspire, persuade, and control. Throughout, students ask: What is the power of language?

OUR CLASS WILL READ AND VIEW THESE TEXTS:

Novel (Literary)

- *Animal Farm*, George Orwell

Poetry

- "'B' (If I Should Have a Daughter," Sarah Kay (text and video)
- "'Hope' is the thing with feathers—," Emily Dickinson (text and video)
- "Dreams," Langston Hughes (text and video)
- "Caged Bird," Maya Angelou (text and video)
- "First They Came for the Communists," Martin Niemoller

Speeches

- Inaugural Address, John F. Kennedy (text and video)
- Address to the United Nations Youth Assembly, Malala Yousafzai (text and video)
- "I Have a Dream," Martin Luther King, Jr. (text and video)

Articles

- "'Ask Not...': JFK's Words Still Inspire 50 Years Later," Nathan Rott
- "Thanks to Malala: Top 3 Ways Malala Has Changed the World," Alex Harris

- "Is Martin Luther King's 'I Have a Dream' the Greatest in History?" Emma Mason
- "How Advertising Targets Our Children," Perri Klass

Historical Accounts

- Excerpts from "Friedrich Engels, Revolutionary, Activist, Unionist, and Social Investigator," Rosalie Baker
- Excerpts from "Grandeur at Abu Simbel," Steven Snape
- Excerpts from "Let's Tour the Temple," Ramadan B. Hussein

Book Reviews

- "In 1946, the *New Republic* Panned George Orwell's *Animal Farm*," George Soule
- Review of *Animal Farm*, Michael Berry
- Review of *Animal Farm*, Bapalapa2, student reviewer
- "Why You Should Read *Animal Farm*," Kainzow, blogger

Video

- Video versions of poems and speeches
- Mini BIO–Joseph Stalin

Advertisements

Propaganda Posters

OUR CLASS WILL VIEW PHOTOGRAPHS OF ANCIENT ARCHITECTURE AND SCULPTURE:

- The Temple at Abu Simbel
- Great Sphinx at Giza

OUR CLASS WILL ASK THESE QUESTIONS:

1. How and why does language inspire?
2. How and why does language persuade?
3. How and why is language dangerous?
4. How and why does language influence thought and action?

QUESTION TO ASK AT HOME:

As your Grade 7 student reads, ask:

- What is the essential meaning, or most important message, in *Animal Farm*?

BOOKS TO READ AT HOME:

- *The Family Romanov: Murder, Rebellion, and the Fall of Imperial Russia*, Candace Fleming
- *Joseph Stalin*, Sean McCollum
- *Breaking Stalin's Nose*, Eugene Yelchin
- *The Wall: Growing Up Behind the Iron Curtain*, Peter Sís
- *Between Shades of Gray*, Ruta Sepetys
- *Stalin: Russia's Man of Steel*, Albert Marrin

IDEAS FOR DISCUSSING THE POWER OF LANGUAGE:

Spend some time together reading poetry, looking through the newspaper or a magazine, watching a political debate or political commercial, or looking at Internet content. Identify examples of language being used to inspire emotion, persuade, or control. Ask questions such as:

1. For poetry: What feelings does the poem inspire? What words, phrases, and images are especially powerful?

2. For advertisements: How is the advertiser trying to persuade us? What techniques does the advertisement use?

3. For politicians: What is the politician trying to convince us of or inspire us to believe? Are these appeals grounded in pathos, logos, or ethos?

4. For all content: What is the message beneath the words? Who is the intended audience and what is the intended purpose?

CREDITS

Great Minds® has made every effort to obtain permission for the reprinting of all copyrighted material. If any owner of copyrighted material is not acknowledged herein, please contact Great Minds® for proper acknowledgment in all future editions and reprints of this module.

- All material from the *Common Core State Standards for English Language Arts & Literacy in History/Social Studies, Science, and Technical Subjects* © Copyright 2010 National Governors Association Center for Best Practices and Council of Chief State School Officers. All rights reserved.

- All images are used under license from Shutterstock.com unless otherwise noted.

- Handout 16B: "Friedrich Engels, Revolutionary, Activist, Unionist, and Social Investigator" by Rosalie Baker from 30 *People Who Changed the World*, Calliope Magazine, January 2011. Text copyright © 2011 by Carus Publishing Company. Reprinted by permission of Cricket Media. All Cricket Media material is copyrighted by Carus Publishing d/b/a Cricket Media, and/or various authors and illustrators. Any commercial use or distribution of material without permission is strictly prohibited. Please visit http://www.cricketmedia.com/info/licensing2 for licensing and http://www.cricketmedia.com for subscriptions.

- Handout 25A: "Let's Tour the Temple" by Ramadan B. Hussein from *Abu Simbel*, Dig Magazine, October 2010. Text copyright © 2010 by Carus Publishing Company. Reprinted by permission of Cricket Media. All Cricket Media material is copyrighted by Carus Publishing d/b/a Cricket Media, and/or various authors and illustrators. Any commercial use or distribution of material without permission is strictly prohibited. Please visit http://www.cricketmedia.com/info/licensing2 for licensing and http://www.cricketmedia.com for subscriptions.

- Handout 25A: "Grandeur at Abu Simbel" by Steven Snape from *Egypt's Ramesses the Great*, Calliope Magazine, October 2005. Text copyright © 2005 by Carus Publishing Company. Reprinted by permission of Cricket Media. All Cricket Media material is copyrighted by Carus Publishing d/b/a Cricket Media, and/or various authors and illustrators. Any commercial use or distribution of material without permission is strictly prohibited. Please visit http://www.cricketmedia.com/info/licensing2 for licensing and http://www.cricketmedia.com for subscriptions.

- For updated credit information, please visit http://witeng.link/credits.

ACKNOWLEDGMENTS

Great Minds® Staff

The following writers, editors, reviewers, and support staff contributed to the development of this curriculum.

Ann Brigham, Lauren Chapalee, Sara Clarke, Emily Climer, Lorraine Griffith, Emily Gula, Sarah Henchey, Trish Huerster, Stephanie Kane-Mainier, Lior Klirs, Liz Manolis, Andrea Minich, Lynne Munson, Marya Myers, Rachel Rooney, Aaron Schifrin, Danielle Shylit, Rachel Stack, Sarah Turnage, Michelle Warner, Amy Wierzbicki, Margaret Wilson, and Sarah Woodard.

Colleagues and Contributors

We are grateful for the many educators, writers, and subject-matter experts who made this program possible.

David Abel, Robin Agurkis, Elizabeth Bailey, Julianne Barto, Amy Benjamin, Andrew Biemiller, Charlotte Boucher, Sheila Byrd-Carmichael, Eric Carey, Jessica Carloni, Janine Cody, Rebecca Cohen, Elaine Collins, Tequila Cornelious, Beverly Davis, Matt Davis, Thomas Easterling, Jeanette Edelstein, Kristy Ellis, Moira Clarkin Evans, Charles Fischer, Marty Gephart, Kath Gibbs, Natalie Goldstein, Christina Gonzalez, Mamie Goodson, Nora Graham, Lindsay Griffith, Brenna Haffner, Joanna Hawkins, Elizabeth Haydel, Steve Hettleman, Cara Hoppe, Ashley Hymel, Carol Jago, Jennifer Johnson, Mason Judy, Gail Kearns, Shelly Knupp, Sarah Kushner, Shannon Last, Suzanne Lauchaire, Diana Leddy, David Liben, Farren Liben, Jennifer Marin, Susannah Maynard, Cathy McGath, Emily McKean, Jane Miller, Rebecca Moore, Cathy Newton, Turi Nilsson, Julie Norris, Galemarie Ola, Michelle Palmieri, Meredith Phillips, Shilpa Raman, Tonya Romayne, Emmet Rosenfeld, Jennifer Ruppel, Mike Russoniello, Deborah Samley, Casey Schultz, Renee Simpson, Rebecca Sklepovich, Amelia Swabb, Kim Taylor, Vicki Taylor, Melissa Thomson, Lindsay Tomlinson, Melissa Vail, Keenan Walsh, Julia Wasson, Lynn Welch, Yvonne Guerrero Welch, Emily Whyte, Lynn Woods, and Rachel Zindler.

Early Adopters

The following early adopters provided invaluable insight and guidance for Wit & Wisdom:

- Bourbonnais School District 53 • Bourbonnais, IL
- Coney Island Prep Middle School • Brooklyn, NY
- Gate City Charter School for the Arts • Merrimack, NH
- Hebrew Academy for Special Children • Brooklyn, NY
- Paris Independent Schools • Paris, KY
- Saydel Community School District • Saydel, IA
- Strive Collegiate Academy • Nashville, TN
- Valiente College Preparatory Charter School • South Gate, CA
- Voyageur Academy • Detroit, MI

Design Direction provided by Alton Creative, Inc.

Project management support, production design, and copyediting services provided by ScribeConcepts.com

Copyediting services provided by Fine Lines Editing

Product management support provided by Sandhill Consulting